THE DEFINITION OF WAR

By Elijah Alexander

Print information available on the last page

Rev. date: 09/13/2018

To order additional copies of this book, contact:
Xlibris
1-888-795-4274
www.Xlibris.com
Orders@Xlibris.com

To whom it may concern.

This book shall end all wars temporarily.

For the Lord of Hosts would say unto thee, Bargain not that this book is incorrect.

For the Lord of Hosts would say unto thee, Free thyself in the truth.

For the Lord of Hosts would say unto thee, Camp thyself on this Freedom.

For the Lord of Hosts would say unto thee, All wars shall end if gone by this book.

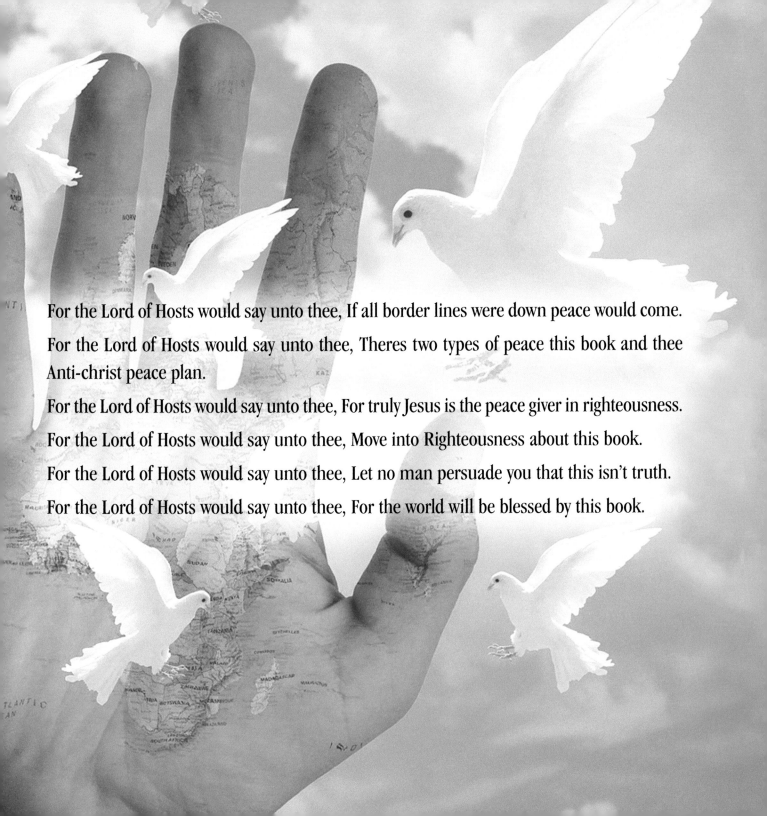

For the Lord of Hosts would say unto thee, If all border lines were down peace would come.

For the Lord of Hosts would say unto thee, Theres two types of peace this book and thee Anti-christ peace plan.

For the Lord of Hosts would say unto thee, For truly Jesus is the peace giver in righteousness.

For the Lord of Hosts would say unto thee, Move into Righteousness about this book.

For the Lord of Hosts would say unto thee, Let no man persuade you that this isn't truth.

For the Lord of Hosts would say unto thee, For the world will be blessed by this book.

For the Lord of Hosts would say unto thee, peace cometh

For the Lord of Hosts would say unto thee, There's a right way for Peace and there's a wrong way for Peace.

For the Lord of Hosts would say unto thee, Come join that righteous Army of Peace makers.

For the Lord of Hosts would say unto thee, Sing a song unto the Lord, peace cometh.

For the Lord of Hosts would say unto thee, This book is a guide to peace.

For the Lord of Hosts would say unto thee, This book shall work.

For the Lord of Hosts would say unto thee, This book is only a temporarily peace plan.

For the Lord of Hosts would say unto thee, The sooner we agree the sooner it will be done.

For the Lord of Hosts would say unto thee, By this book so shall the world be strengthened.

For the Lord of Hosts would say unto thee, Take charge by going by this book.

For the Lord of Hosts would say unto thee, the sooner the better.

For the Lord of Hosts would say unto thee, Let this book be a hand guide for Peace.

For the Lord of Hosts would say unto thee, Accept this book in the now.

For the Lord of Hosts would say unto thee, Peace be upon thee now.

For the Lord of Hosts would say unto thee, come join that righteous Army of Peace.

For the Lord of Hosts would say unto thee, Be blessed.

For the Lord of Hosts would say unto thee, Be still and know that I am God.

For the Lord of Hosts would say unto thee, Strengthen one another by this book.

For the Lord of Hosts would say unto thee, Be smart and go by this book.

For the Lord of Hosts would say unto thee, This is the 2nd best book about peace, the Bible is first.

For the Lord of Hosts would say unto thee, Let's see what the Lord can do.

For the Lord of Hosts would say unto thee, Thee army of the Lord are peace makers.

For the Lord of Hosts would say unto thee, Congratulations Army of the Lord peace is coming.

For the Lord of Hosts would say unto thee, miracles are in the now for peace.

For the Lord of Hosts would say unto thee, Wisdom is found in the Bible peace is apart of it.

For the Lord of Hosts would say unto thee, Money cannot buy peace, but the Bible can.

For the Lord of Hosts would say unto thee, Speak peace with this book and it will increase.

For the Lord of Hosts would say unto thee, Special are the peace makers.

For the Lord of Hosts would say unto thee, God has granted peace by this book.

For the Lord of Hosts would say unto thee, Strength does not ly in war but peace.

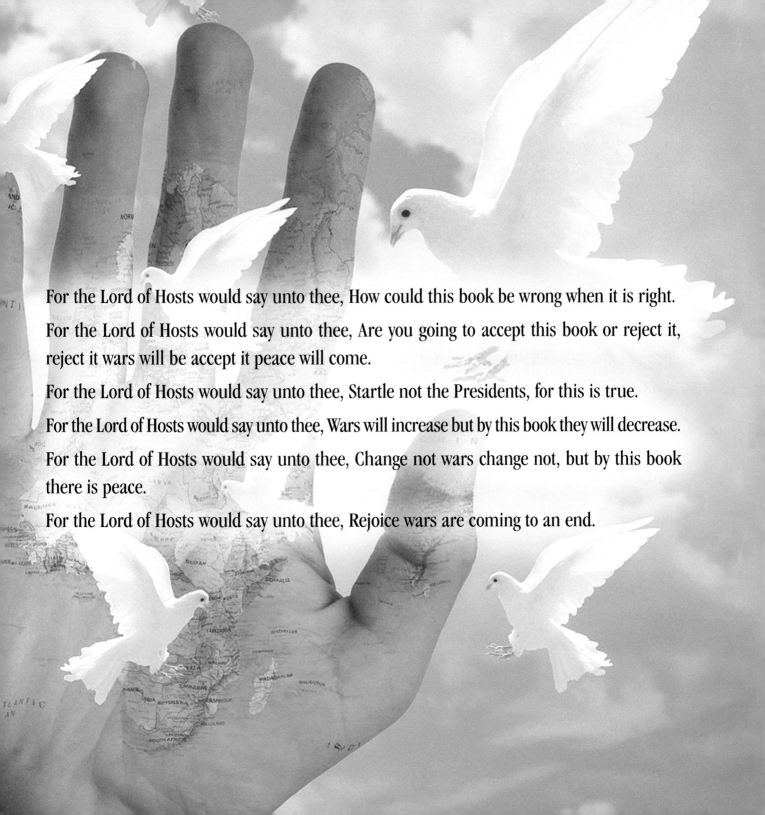

For the Lord of Hosts would say unto thee, How could this book be wrong when it is right.

For the Lord of Hosts would say unto thee, Are you going to accept this book or reject it, reject it wars will be accept it peace will come.

For the Lord of Hosts would say unto thee, Startle not the Presidents, for this is true.

For the Lord of Hosts would say unto thee, Wars will increase but by this book they will decrease.

For the Lord of Hosts would say unto thee, Change not wars change not, but by this book there is peace.

For the Lord of Hosts would say unto thee, Rejoice wars are coming to an end.

For the Lord of Hosts would say unto thee, Wisdom says this book is right.

For the Lord of Hosts would say unto thee, believe and ye shall receive.

For the Lord of Hosts would say unto thee, This is a good book.

For the Lord of Hosts would say unto thee, Christ is ready for peace how about you.

For the Lord of Hosts would say unto thee, Get along with each other about this book.

For the Lord of Hosts would say unto thee, When doing this book stay in God's will.

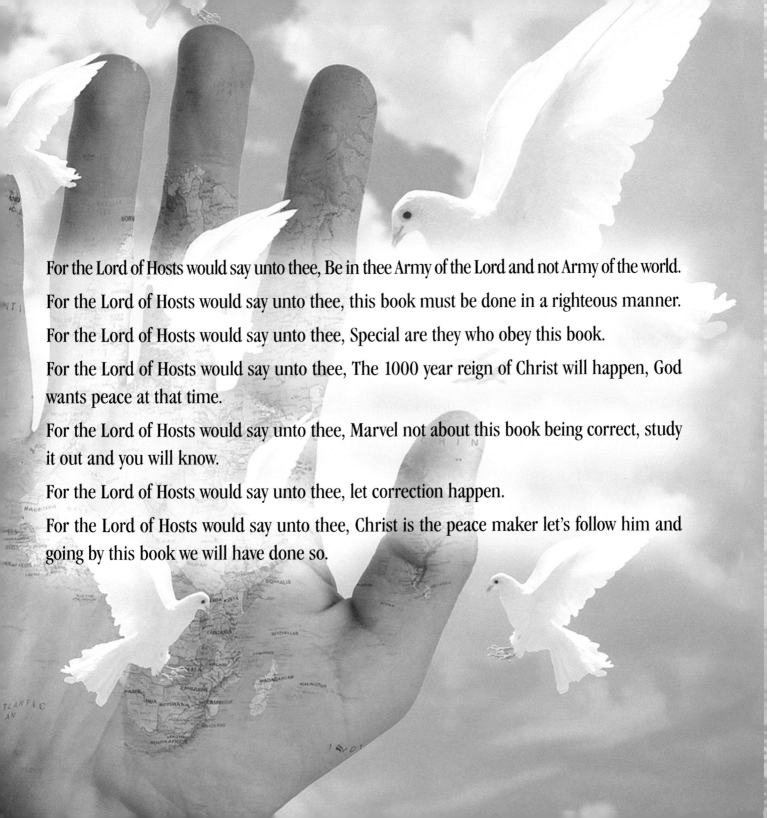

For the Lord of Hosts would say unto thee, Be in thee Army of the Lord and not Army of the world.

For the Lord of Hosts would say unto thee, this book must be done in a righteous manner.

For the Lord of Hosts would say unto thee, Special are they who obey this book.

For the Lord of Hosts would say unto thee, The 1000 year reign of Christ will happen, God wants peace at that time.

For the Lord of Hosts would say unto thee, Marvel not about this book being correct, study it out and you will know.

For the Lord of Hosts would say unto thee, let correction happen.

For the Lord of Hosts would say unto thee, Christ is the peace maker let's follow him and going by this book we will have done so.

For the Lord of Hosts would say unto thee, my name is Elijah and I can answer every Question about this book.

For the Lord of Hosts would say unto thee, Special is this book for it came from the Lord.

For the Lord of Hosts would say unto thee, the military shall be set free.

For the Lord of Hosts would say unto thee, Strength and power are in this book.

For the Lord of Hosts would say unto thee, This book is healing and relief.

For the Lord of Hosts would say unto thee, The military worldwide shall be set free.

For the Lord of Hosts would say unto thee, Common sense tells you this book is right.

For the Lord of Hosts would say unto thee, a mighty move of God is about to take place.

For the Lord of Hosts would say unto thee, a great fiasco is about healed, war.

For the Lord of Hosts would say unto thee, capture that right Spirit about this.

For the Lord of Hosts would say unto thee, Hallelujah God reigneth.

For the Lord of Hosts would say unto thee, soon and temporarily all wars shall cease.

For the Lord of Hosts would say unto thee, A temporary one world Government is going to happen.

For the Lord of Hosts would say unto thee, March in the Lord's will when this happens.

For the Lord of Hosts would say unto thee, capture that right Spirit in prayer.

For the Lord of Hosts would say unto thee, There's going to be changes in thee earth.

For the Lord of Hosts would say unto thee, There's going to be a temporarily better Government.

For the Lord of Hosts would say unto thee, This government will not last long.

For the Lord of Hosts would say unto thee, Pray about this so you will understand.

For the Lord of Hosts would say unto thee, Do not reject this book in unrighteousness.

For the Lord of Hosts would say unto thee, what does the Bible have'ft to say about this book.

For the Lord of Hosts would say unto thee, Rejoice this is a righteous book.

For the Lord of Hosts would say unto thee, Jesus is that righteous government.

For the Lord of Hosts would say unto thee, The spirit of the Lord is in this.

For the Lord of Hosts would say unto thee, Do not take this book lightly.

For the Lord of Hosts would say unto thee, If this book is gone by righteousness, righteousness will prevail.

For the Lord of Hosts would say unto thee, Study this book out.

For the Lord of Hosts would say unto thee, Jesus is the peace giver in righteousness.

For the Lord of Hosts would say unto thee, Be friendly about this book.

For the Lord of Hosts would say unto thee, The right thing will happen about this book.

For the Lord of Hosts would say unto thee, True happiness is coming about war.

For the Lord of Hosts would say unto thee, If you do this book prayerfully you will know this book is correct.

For the Lord of Hosts would say unto thee, Come join that righteous Army of peace.

For the Lord of Hosts would say unto thee, Wars are about to cease.

For the Lord of Hosts would say unto thee, Some major problems in the world are about to end.

For the Lord of Hosts would say unto thee, Strength is in the Lord and that includes peace.

For the Lord of Hosts would say unto thee, A great miracle is about to happen, Peace.

For the Lord of Hosts would say unto thee. A breakthrough is about to take place, war.

For the Lord of Hosts would say unto thee, Strength is Love and strength is peace.

For the Lord of Hosts would say unto thee, Peace is in the Bible.

For the Lord of Hosts would say unto thee, Love is peace and it's a great thing to do.

For the Lord of Hosts would say unto thee, Pray right things will happen.

For the Lord of Hosts would say unto thee, great blessings follow them who do this book righteously.

For the Lord of Hosts would say unto thee, The right thing is going to happen about this book.

For the Lord of Hosts would say unto thee, Contentions will happen.

For the Lord of Hosts would say unto thee, Jesus is the peace maker give him the praise.

For the Lord of Hosts would say unto thee, peace is God's will.

For the Lord of Hosts would say unto thee ???

For the Lord of Hosts would say unto thee, Peace cometh which means great deliverance.

For the Lord of Hosts would say unto thee, Great blessings are about to happen because of peace.

For the Lord of Hosts would say unto thee, Strength is in war. Strength is in peace, choose peace.

For the Lord of Hosts would say unto thee, The Bible speaks of peace accept it.

For the Lord of Hosts would say unto thee, Be on the winning team, Peace.

For the Lord of Hosts would say unto thee, The master reigneth and he is for peace.

For the Lord of Hosts would say unto thee, Congratulations peace makers you've done a great thing.

For the Lord of Hosts would say unto thee, Smile God loves you.

For the Lord of Hosts would say unto thee, Because he is real peace is real.

For the Lord of Hosts would say unto thee, If there is no borders there's no need for nuclear weapons.

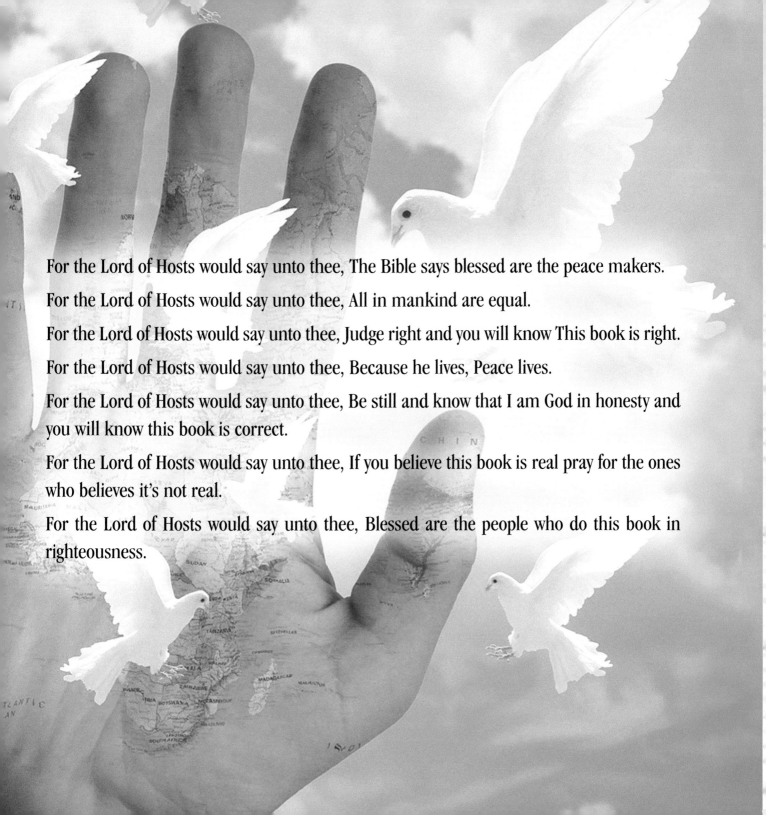

For the Lord of Hosts would say unto thee, The Bible says blessed are the peace makers.

For the Lord of Hosts would say unto thee, All in mankind are equal.

For the Lord of Hosts would say unto thee, Judge right and you will know This book is right.

For the Lord of Hosts would say unto thee, Because he lives, Peace lives.

For the Lord of Hosts would say unto thee, Be still and know that I am God in honesty and you will know this book is correct.

For the Lord of Hosts would say unto thee, If you believe this book is real pray for the ones who believes it's not real.

For the Lord of Hosts would say unto thee, Blessed are the people who do this book in righteousness.

Printed in the United States
By Bookmasters